Visions Of The Daughters Of

Albion

Emily S. Hamblen

Kessinger Publishing's Rare Reprints

Thousands of Scarce and Hard-to-Find Books on These and other Subjects!

- Americana
- Ancient Mysteries
- Animals
- Anthropology
- Architecture
- Arts
- Astrology
- Bibliographies
- Biographies & Memoirs
- Body, Mind & Spirit
- Business & Investing
- Children & Young Adult
- Collectibles
- Comparative Religions
- Crafts & Hobbies
- Earth Sciences
- Education
- Ephemera
- Fiction
- Folklore
- Geography
- Health & Diet
- History
- Hobbies & Leisure
- Humor
- Illustrated Books
- Language & Culture
- Law
- Life Sciences
- Literature
- Medicine & Pharmacy
- Metaphysical
- Music
- Mystery & Crime
- Mythology
- Natural History
- Outdoor & Nature
- Philosophy
- Poetry
- Political Science
- Science
- Psychiatry & Psychology
- Reference
- Religion & Spiritualism
- Rhetoric
- Sacred Books
- Science Fiction
- Science & Technology
- Self-Help
- Social Sciences
- Symbolism
- Theatre & Drama
- Theology
- Travel & Explorations
- War & Military
- Women
- Yoga
- *Plus Much More!*

We kindly invite you to view our catalog list at:
http://www.kessinger.net

VISIONS: The daughters of Albion are seen *weeping* because they are *enslaved*. Weeping is the instinctive response of the subconscious, or the memory portion of being, to an intellectual perception; accompanied by a consciousness of inability to act in response to the incitement of the perception. As when one is stirred by a sudden comprehension of the meaning of bygone emotional experiences without developing power of will to act in accordance with the light the perception brings. There is only *trembling lamentation* upon the outlook—*the mountains*—and a *sighing toward* the enlarged consciousness that might be realized. But no action, because the intellectual powers are not yet sufficiently developed. Lacking this intellectual alliance which she should have found in Theotormon, Oothoon *wanders in woe, seeking flowers to comfort her*. She will content herself, perforce, with nature's ultimate expression—the flowering in the finer sentiments of human life of those impulses which men share with all other natural beings. But this is not unity; creative power; the *humanity which is above sex*. Blake, as possessor of the artist soul, was committed to the necessity of spontaneous expression. As one who never had submitted his will and spirit to the rule of any established order, while he yet passionately sought harmony—*loved Theotormon*—he inevitably looked for the principle of unity in that impulse to creative expression which prompts every living thing to maintain its own type. For man, who must find himself through understanding of the world in which he moves, whose typical characteristic is the power to create through imagination—therefore in the spiritual world—it is of prime importance to know what essentially is the consummation of the life in nature.

Let us illustrate: The unthinking man can marry from the instinct to form domestic ties, will love his wife and children, work for them laboriously, leave them with better facilities for meeting the world successfully than he himself enjoyed, and die content with his achievement. But the spiritual man—above all, the genius—has found within himself something that stands apart in even the most intimate relationships of life. Something which he may lose through these relationships but may not gain unless he understands whether or not they tend toward a spiritual goal and what this goal may be. Such a man does not merge his personality in the company with which he travels through life but interrogates the quality of the bond at every instant. At the moment in Blake's life when these visions were written, Blake unquestionably felt his genius to be threatened by some dictation from the outward world; or at the least by an expectation that he would conform to the ordinary ways of the men of his time. His very soul was menaced as its right to spontaneous action was questioned, and all the passion of a repression whose results his imagination could draw, flows out into musical lamentation in this poem. That it could be not only musical but melodious, proves the depth and the sincerity of Blake's spiritual wrestling.

The *Marygold of Leutha's vale* is that union of the basic opposites of the earth life which is accomplished in the spiritual experiences that accompany and emanate from the impulses of sex; as the gentler sentiment of humanity, especially the spirit of devotion and self-sacrifice toward the child. Also, that power to know beauty which we believe to be a distinctively human attribute—perhaps mistakenly so. Is this lure to life which nature holds out to man a consummation—*a flower*—or is it an emotional formative principle active within the phenomenon—a *nymph*? It is suggestive that the transmutable part of the caterpillar is termed *nymph*. The soul aspiring to a still larger consciousness of nature is fearful of dividing from their source in nature the values that nature gives. To isolate phenomena for one's delight would seem a condemnation of nature. Oothoon *dared not pluck the flower from its dewy bed*. No, this is not the attitude toward the physical world of the artist in whom the love of nature has grown with his growth and strengthened with his strength. That is *a sweet delight*—a part of soul growth interwoven with the consciousness of higher soul powers which are seeking to come forth. The nymph is *golden*—essential. The spiritual in the natural is just that desire to create in which power concentrates, and the flower exists as a potential culmination in the force of this desire. Let us note here the fearlessness with which the seer and the mystic accept desire as the basic fact of existence. The ancients presented it under some of their finest, as well as under violent, symbols. Jacob Boehme openly names the flame of the life impulse *lust*, interpreting this in accordance with its etymological connections, as the urge of energy to free itself from confining bonds. Blake and Nietzsche are at one in finding it essential to all values, while recognizing that it may not become its counterpart, will without action upon it of the spiritual or intellectual principle. In this view of life the mystic, supposed to be a pale abstractionist, stands apart from the metaphysician, however human the philosophy of the latter may be. For the unity achieved by the metaphysician takes place in the conceptual world, while the world of nature is looked upon as hostile to the forces which move in the higher sphere. "Not so," says the mystic. "This duality of nature is in spirit itself, together with the urge toward unity." When passion is creative, higher form results. When, through restraint, passion is dark; blind to its own meaning as the creative energy of the universe; seeking to satisfy its trouble through dominance rather than through union; then arise sensuality, terrors, devastating hostilities. Then men begin to call passion *evil*, blind to the fact that it is restraint of the impulse to act, to create, which is the evil thing. Why is it that the higher, purer spirits among men have acclaimed desire and passion while the great majority of mankind—including most of the philosophers—have consigned it to the realm of devildom? Is it not just because the passion in themselves has been so rare, so refined, and so undeniable a force at the centre of consciousness that they have comprehended it as very spirit? How have we distorted words, so that no longer we can understand those who use them in a virginal sense? *Force* to our ears, even *power*, means nothing but brute strength. *Passion* means physical desire. In reality the lower cravings have no strength, no power of convulsion in comparison with spiritual passion. The former are blind, ineffectual wanderers. The latter is the shaping fire ever becoming visible in forms of progressive beauty and beneficence. The voluptuary burns out in body and in spirit. The saint, the idealist, the genius burn on as living flames at the heart of humanity.

There need be therefore no dread of this fact of contraries which is the enkindler of passion. It is a very condition of one kind of delight, and as such it has a permanent place in the cosmic order. Only the mind that has debased nature to its own low level sees opposites as mutually destructive. On the other hand, nature has her own specific place and must speak her piece only in accordance with her power of discernment. The soul of man has other departments and having conceived itself in this elementary one it must inquire more deeply concerning itself from the vantage point of a higher level of consciousness. Therefore *the golden nymph*, after yielding up her thought and her flower, *ceases and closes her shrine*.

Oothoon is the soul aspiring to full consciousness—to complete use and understanding of its powers; taking into its emotional life the spiritual import of Nature's realm and, thus started on her career, *turning her face* toward realization. The syllabic formation of the word proves that it is the temperamental department of the soul—the Capricornus stage of aspiration striving for individual consciousness and definition—which is intended. For the sound *oo*, repeated with its resonator *n*, is one which sets in vibration the abdominal muscles more thoroughly perhaps than any other combination of sounds. The aim of the Hebrew discipline through art was to make the body a harp; healthy and sound in instinct so that it would respond to the touch of spirit. David as the supreme exponent of the emotional life of the people was the harpist.

But at this point we may pertinently ask how do Thel and Oothoon differ? Thel is the Romantic Beauty which seeks continuance and evolution only in the elemental. She has to learn that in the elemental itself resides no power to transmute into continuing spiritual values. Only service is there, implying aspiration, but blind in its nature. Power to lift the natural above its own plane exists only in the creative energy of a soul which has found itself and thus found the law of the universe, either through struggle or through a perpetual, untouched virginity of vision. This struggle Thel evaded. She chose the gloss. Oothoon holds on to the essential in nature but strives toward intellectual perception. It must also be noted that four years had elapsed between the composition of the two poems. Blake has moved along on the road of enlightenment and his vision is more inclusive.

Confidence in life and the world as essentially ideal is the cause of exultation. It carries the soul as on wings *over the waves* of conceivable being. Foundations being sure, all that is reared above them must be of transcendent value. As love in human life which awakens the sense of the eternal seems the earnest of a purer and an immortal existence. But disastrously for these winged flights of the soul, the course which it must take over the waves lies through the realm of man's rationalistic effort to reduce the elemental stuff of life to a harmony. It is the very idealism of the soul which makes inevitable a critical meeting with that prevailing moral order which the general soul has decreed as a frame for holding the picture of the cosmos. So Oothoon is not preserved from this meeting by the strong impetus which she received from Nature known under its sublimated aspects, but finds her force overcome by that impulse of the dual nature which prompts the activities of Theotormon. This meeting is Bromion; the stormy rage of the elemental nature divided against itself by a restraint which it cannot understand nor justify. The *terror* which it exerts over the soul exists, however, unmistakably. The attempts to overcome the tension form the bulk of man's moral consciousness. Combat is inevitable. It is the great discipline of the soul nurtured on the Indo-European culture. As a high representative of this culture, who yet was born to apprehension of life on a more exalted plane, Blake submitted to this discipline to the full. Not a long time after the visions were written Blake, as we have seen, came to a clearer understanding of the necessity of systems which involve a degree of restraint and became less rebellious against them. But at this point he could see nothing but a violation of man's spirit—a crippling of his genius—in laws which the human reason had framed. It will be well to remind ourselves here that some six or eight years before the date and the vision, Blake lost the light that enlightened his youth; that mystic radiance from the heart of things which falls upon the child eye, wide open in uncritical wonder—initial prerequisite of comprehension. Whether in his art activities or his personal life or both, this open attitude of the artist had come hard up against the conventions of the time and in the encounter had had its wings clipped. If repression and perversion of individual talent are a source of distress to the average man and woman, what must be the agony of spirit in the case of a fiery genius like Blake? What other relief should such a spirit seek than to lift the phenomena of his own experience to the cosmic

plane? Discerning readers of *Also Sprach Zarathustra* have some-
times been almost shocked at learning the apparently trivial
circumstances which gave rise to some of the author's greatest
thoughts. But it is not the *occasion* of an outburst of energy which
is the fact of importance; it is the quantum of force which has
accumulated and awaits a form in which it may find an organic
release. It is as with women; to some a mere touch of the hand
inspired only by the sex impulse, where a spiritual relation had
been believed in, will cause deeper suffering and mental confusion
than betrayal and social disgrace will bring to others. It is the
plane of consciousness upon which such things occur that is of
prime significance. Or, as Blake would say, the *state* which the
soul inhabits at the moment.

Oothoon's first child, then, was not to be an Edenic birth but
the offspring of moral struggle. The demand that divine unity be
found within a system which Reason alone had framed, proceeding
on the assumption of an evil principle at the heart of nature, has
destroyed the virginity of the soul. Bromion proclaims his conquest
and offers to Theotormon only a deflowered bride and an illegitimate
child. The soul has lost assurance of the innocence of its prompt-
ings. They spring from an unresolvable duality, the raging elemental
nature declares, while bound in its *caves*; lost in instincts and desires
which have no creative direction. *Let the jealous dolphins sport
around the lovely maid.* That is, let the elemental forms of jealousy
—chief expression of hostile opposites—make sport of the simplicity
which belongs to the maiden outlook—the perception of innocence
at the heart of nature. For, instigated by the dual consciousness,
creation falls to the level of generation. And the impulse to
generation is not the creative aspiration toward a new unity, but
the lure of sex. Ino, mother of Heracles—great hero of the
dual struggle—turned into a dolphin and passed through the waters
with an infant at her breast. *Dolphin* analysed means *to beget,
to generate through the lure* (*dolos* and *phen*, from *phio*).

In reality all impulse is imparted by Bromion. Theotormon
must understand this and *protect the child*—the resulting philosophy
of life—which Oothoon *shall put forth in nine months' time*; arrive
at after a full gestation period in that world of man's manifestation
wherein he seeks to reflect the eternal.

Blake has given us two pictures, a pen and a brush, equally

vivid, of Theotormon's despairing rage over the forced union of Oothoon with Bromion. It is the divine genius of man, needing to find the God-like everywhere, but convinced that the natural lies outside of the ideal realm; thereby forcing the rational faculty to suppress the elemental portion of personality because this threatens the only structure that the soul has been strong enough and comprehending enough to erect.

In the design Theotormon has lost human semblance. The limbs are wreathed round the head, hiding all but the crown. The right hand and foot—agents of the mind—are concealed. The left foot —emotional side of the body—is grossly misshapen; the left hand clutches the hair. It also is misshapen; the thumb is unformed and the fingers end at the first joint and resemble the teeth of a rake or a saw. Imagery found in other poems of Blake, as well as possible etymological connotations, suggests that the form of the left hand was meant to express limitation of the emotional life to the vision of the Church. Already I had found the term *priest* in the verb *eprisa* (*prio*)—*to saw asunder*. Blake certainly had the same idea.

Bromion, *back to back* with Oothoon, holding her by her arms with his own arms stretched behind him, while Oothoon's head falls forward and those breasts which had taken to themselves the flower of the golden nymph show the tension of the grasp within which she is held—Bromion is weighted to the earth by a chain around the ankles which runs into an iron ring. His will is bound to that ring of recurrence which is inseparable from the consciousness limited to the dual conception of life. Over the waves which lie behind the group, the clouds suggest by their form the primordial bird which lays the cyclic egg; in Egyptian lore, the goose Seb. The rayless sun, as an egg just dropped from the rock-like nest upon which the bird sits, stands in a space enclosed by seven curved lines. It is Blake's own mental picture of what the soul of man in this age has been able to draw out of the elements of the universe.

In the verse, *Theotormon rolls his waves and folds his black waters round the adulterate pair*; note the term. Theology has enfolded in its cosmic plan the concept of the antagonism of opposites. These opposites become two mental attitudes; one terror, the rage of restraint, and fear at the rage; the other meekness—a spirit of concession inevitable when the soul is bound to terror.

But this is the subterranean life; instinctive. Theotormon *sits at the threshold* (note the modern term), *wearing it away with secret tears.* The reason which the soul striving for unity employs is not enlightened. Its processes of attrition upon the dividing line between instinct and mind are not clear. Religion through its repressions creates *slaves beneath the sun.* It *traffics* in the hopes of men—*their children*—and these *shiver in the caves* which lie beneath *the burning fires of lust that belch incessant from the summits of the earth.* That is, the passions which it has been the purpose of religion to subdue, turned to sensuality by coercion, exhibit their lower nature in the institutions of religion—the summits of the earth.

But though Theotormon *weeps, Oothoon cannot.* The emotional life has become thoroughly chilled by being discredited and is *locked up.* Its utterances are not articulate, affirmative, harmonious. They are the distressed voice of struggle with an inner chaos. The soul must have help from the perceiving intellect. The intellect must be urged to attain to perfection through exercise of the powers of the genius. Let these *prey upon* what may be *fleshly* in the soul's relation to the natural.

Oothoon *calls with holy voice*—an utterance of the whole being— for purification. It is only *the kings of the sounding air* who can *rend away her defiled bosom* and make it transparent for the reflection of the image of Theotormon. What is this? Intellectual integrity is a pure thing, however limited it may be. It is not won except through abnegation and excision of much which appeals to the sensitive nature with comfort and charm. What is retained and affirmed has passed through the fire of drastic criticism. Theotormon's smile at Oothoon is a *severe* one. *Kings* are dominant, organizing ideas. The *sounding air* is the rarer, so-called etheric, medium which carries sound to the inner ear. In *Vala*, Blake looks back to the ancient time when earth had her place in an *auricular universe.* That is, a universal order in which the inhabitants of the earth plane were in communication with other planes through sensitiveness of the inner ear to vibrations of the general medium. Blake did not argue from his own possession of this higher power that he was an advanced member of an evolving race. Rather he contended that the higher men as a class had possessed the greater power in ancient times. And this he argued from the evidences for his belief which he found in the ancient scriptures. Nietzsche must have meant the same thing when he said that the words of Zarathustra were *shouted at him* and that he doubted whether any other man had been so inspired for ten thousand years. The archæologists were then giving civilization no such term as that.

Therefore, in a crisis which threatened the ideal nature of the soul in its very foundation, whither shall it turn for the salvation of its holiest values except to that higher self, that individual genius which is something apart from the five senses and all that can be apprehended by them? The powers of genius—the higher activities of the personality—leave their native element of clarity and assurance and descend to the rescue of the soul. Though the purification process is a severe one, it is reconciling, and the soul that welcomes the rending which causes it to bleed, becomes again as *a clear spring*— cleansed from the subhuman emotions—*feet of the beasts*—which had invaded it. Nevertheless the suffering entailed by the experience affects the emotional nature, altering it in its elements.

But still the soul and the rational understanding cannot unite, even though the soul has been purified of the fleshly taint, and both soul and mind tragically feel the need of unity. The soul knows that the intellect must come into union with her. Intellect cannot perceive that unity should be attained through alliance with the struggle-nature. For therein is duality, and where there are opposites one or the other must be impure. Thus avers Reason, the loquacious part of intellect.

There are times in the history of the race when the emotional life is strong and the rational life is not sufficiently developed to meet it. There are other times when the reverse is true. "The Son of Man hath not where to lay his head," said Jesus. The human mind in his time had been trained to the splitting of hairs, but spiritual emotion— desire for the higher experienced life of the spirit and a true sentiment of humanity—was wanting. The wishes of the common people were directed toward material things. The intellectual classes were lost in political wisdom, dialectic or conceptualism. There had been no corresponding expansion of the emotional life. But in the age of Blake the emotional needs of man were acutely felt. The passional nature was strong notwithstanding the surface conventionalism. To match it there should have been a development of intellect to the point of complete comprehension. Nothing better was offered by the leaders of thought than an arid Deism; itself, Blake believed, nothing more than the Christian morality divested of the forms of the church. Thus Oothoon finds none to listen to her lamentations but Bromion, whose Dionysian impulse, like her own, presses toward new births. Why cannot Theotormon see that all is ready for the descent of intellect into the elemental realm, the conceptual having been left behind? The *village dog barks at the breaking day*—that predatory instinct (wolf) has been tamed and domesticated to a free, but social order—*village* as opposed to the *city*, a completely integrated oversoul. I imagine, too, that there is reference to the customs of the Essenes—the purest spirits of the age immediately preceding the Christian era. It has been thought by some students that Jesus came from the sect. However that may be, its philosophy cannot have failed to influence his thought. The homes of the Essenes were in villages. A true instinct would lead the soul away from a Christianity run to institutions and moralism and make it envisage a life of purification. The village beginning would then flower into the culture of a spiritual city.

The genius of man—*eagle*—has penetrated to man's hidden nature and found somewhat to carry to the pure realm of aspiration. The soul itself has learned that it is not a prisoner, or merely an instrument of the senses, and has emerged from the *deadly black* with which such a belief enshrouded it. But Theotormon has not sensed this passage of the soul from darkness to a dawning light. *Both night and morn*—residual effect of the past and dawn of the future—are alike to him in an absolute materialism and morality; both based on belief in an obdurate physical world and a duality in part evil. There is no avenue of escape for the intellect or the moral nature while life is thus rationalized; nothing but *a night of sighs, a morning of fresh tears*.

But how can even a reason disjoined from spiritual insight fail to see that there is no framework based upon the report of the senses into which the diverse phenomena of life will fit? Let Reason go to the animals and attempt to force them into one group on the basis of all possessing the same senses. This fact of similarity is true, but over and above these senses which all have in common, each species has a sense which is peculiar to its kind alone; a thing *sui generis*; isolated and unique as the genius of man. Let Theotormon ask why each bird and beast is so passionate in its own peculiar way, then tell *what are the thoughts of man that have been hid of old*. For when wisdom has been sought in this way, then the heart will understand more of what the eye perceives. For the spirit of man can know in reality only that which can be brought within the compass of its own power to experience; and if man shall discover something of the life that is expressed in the subhuman form, he shall recover lost parts of his own soul. It has been said of Blake that it is startling to find the principle of evolution in his designs so long before the theory had been advanced. But Blake had taken to himself the larger philosophy of involution and evolution, one succeeding the other in vast cycles, which ancient seers found in the universe.

Oothoon pleads again that because change is at hand, because the soul of man is casting off outworn forms and seeking a new estate it shall be met sympathetically, not regarded as a negligible part of personality. Is it not primarily the emotions which have been *touched by sorrow*; innocence which has felt the taint of impurity; the form culminating in beauty which had its origin in the old earth of the everflowing River of Time, that are the most precious things? In such essences and consummations the soul has *bathed its wings* and is *white and pure* to meet the immaculate intellect. Emotion is thus eloquent but *could be silent* if its nature were comprehended in love. During the night, when the greater mind is active, the soul does not plead. The only critic it has to face is the rational element in mind. Thus in prose we render the exquisite lines in which Oothoon's sorrow sings:

> Silent I hover all the night, and all day could be silent
> If Theotormon once would turn his lov'd eyes upon me.
> How can I be defil'd when I reflect thy image pure?
> Sweetest the fruit that the worm feeds on, and the soul prey'd on by woe;
> The new wash'd lamb ting'd with the village smoke, and the bright swan
> By the red earth of our immortal river. I bathe my wings
> And I am white and pure to hover round Theotormon's breast.

Theotormon, who has remained silent while he folded his dark waves around those parts of personality from which he might have received fresh impulse—the elemental nature of Earth-man struggling with dualism, Bromion, and the soul aspiring to realize unity but dependent upon the conscious mind to make such realization complete; Theotormon now breaks his silence and responds

to Oothoon's challenge and entreaty. She has said that night
and day are both alike to him, whereas each day should be a morn
unlike any other because each night had given new power to the
faculty which works by day. She had asked why he could think a
fixed system could interpret nature while each living thing has a
unique and specific faculty and purpose and manner of finding
delight. She had begged Theotormon to try to understand the
nature of her struggle; to strive to know her as a thing unique
and able to achieve purity only if free to live according to the law
of her own being. But the conscious mind is full of confusion;
unable of itself to throw off the shackles within which it was formed.
It, like Oothoon, needs unity and is o'erflowed with woe from the
want. How can it understand its own nature and content? *What
is a thought? Where do thoughts dwell* before they are called forth
in the struggle of the soul? *What is a joy?* To what manner of
ordered living do joys belong? Where *are* the joys, experienced
but lost? And the loves? Which streams of Time bring sorrow
to man? From what outlooks upon life is only discontent in view;
life's elements in a desperate state? What, in short, is this abiding-
place in which there is only wretchedness and constraint because
of despair? Oh, that the joys and the loves once known might be
renewed! The mind will *traverse times and spaces far remote* from
its habitual course to find this comfort for its *present sorrow and
this night of pain*. But fear and doubt cripple the wings of desire.
Might not the result of such a flight be the discovery that the
origin of life is not to be found in something essential, ethereal,
healing; but in the poison of that instinctive envy which belongs
to the consciousness of the dual nature; explicitly to the hostilities
of the unsublimated sex instinct? Theotormon desires but cannot
act upon his desires because of fear.

Bromion replying *shakes the cavern with his lamentation*. Observe
that *lamentation* is used symbolically only in connection with
elemental things, whether natural or psychic, to express their
inherent futility as agents. The suggestion here is of a will, or
purpose, unillumined—or unrealized—through repression, because
the Reason is enthralled.

Theotormon has wished to send thought back to the ancient
days of belief in joy and love, hoping that it would return with a
message of consolation. Bromion, himself desiring to express his

nature under new forms—to follow the law of transformation, which is the very law of life—reminds Theotormon that he knows already about the fruit of the ancient trees; understands something of the processes by which existing things of the moral world have been generated. What he now needs to know for the relief of his pain is, that the objects which he has come to understand through the medium of the five senses in reality exist to enable him to evolve still other senses. He has perceived; he has not known. One may perceive many things about a friend but come to know him only at some moment when a new consciousness is born; when scales which have covered an inner eye fall away. Thus, and thus only, says Blake, is it with the entire visible world. It is perceived by man, but not with knowledge. For such knowledge one must voyage into another kind of sea. It is a call to go forward to superhumanity, the one escape from the age-long failure of earth.

What an escape it will be from the wheel of Recurrence! *Are there other wars* than those of the sword? Other joys beside the material ones? Other sorrows than the sordid, soul-killing kind? Is it really true that the various natures need not conform to a single law? Can it be that the seeming phantasms of existence really are not doomed by decree to an eternal consuming fire and bound away from an eternal life by an unchanging process?

Theotormon answers not. Oothoon *waited silent all the day and all the night*—contemplating the Bromion thought in all its phases —and speaks only when it has awakened in her a new intelligence —*when the morn arose.* But even so the new thought is cause for renewed lamentation, for Theotormon still has not *turned his eyes* upon the struggle of the soul. *O Urizen!* exclaims Oothoon, with sharp, direct attack upon the very principle and essence of rationalization which is holding Theotormon under its spell; *O Urizen! Creator of men*—making man as you are able to perceive him and allowing him to be nothing more than that. *Mistaken Demon of heaven!* A Demos principle which by mistake has made the ideal world. Putting before man false issues. Pushing him to consummations which have no relation to his eternal destiny. Thy creative action is inspired by impulse which is ineffectual in the spiritual realm—*tears.* Thy labour to form men according to the imagination you have of human nature is a work of vanity! In your creative effort, so called, one fact, incident, personality is categoried under another according to the law that you decree. Thus you build. But this is not true of creation. In the life process each thing stands out by itself—unique, not to be absorbed. Such is the work of Joy. Joy arising from love for that with which it is dealing. And how can one joy absorb another? For joy and love are impossible without belief in simplicity and eternal values. Each thing capable of being a joy is holy—whole—eternal, infinite. The soul knows this. Shall Reason, bent upon devitalizing the world, dominate the soul?

In the interests of systems, human nature has been forced to expression of which it is typically incapable and the meaning of all that is expressed in subhuman nature has been lost through failure to distinguish each type by its function. Gratitude is enjoined upon those who are too low in the moral order to know the meaning of the sentiment. It is expected of the intelligence so narrow that it can only *mock at the labour* which *cannot be paid for in money. How different the eye and the ear* of men whose desires are opposed and whose talents are diverse. How different their worlds. Yet, as though possessed of a special inclusive sense, *the parson* claims the labour of all, as the farmer reaps many kinds of crops—employing all available devices—*into gins and traps*; surrounding himself with abstractions and with things generated—*forests*—to differentiate his humanity, and that of the possessors of political power, from the humanity of the race in general; until his anti-natural values have become impressed upon the mind of his time and the innate genius—the soul which in order to develop must be free—finds itself bound, as one may be bound in a hated marriage bond, and *produces unripe births* from want of time to mature its own thoughts.

Encountering the worlds of beasts and of birds, spiritual discernment is not employed, because insight is destroyed through the desire to describe all forms and processes by means of formulas. Yet even the lowest of the animal creation, *the worm*, may teach man the great and joyful lesson of rebirth. What, in a free world, stands opposed to these formulated schemes of the rational mind? Infancy and Innocence. The fearlessness, impulsiveness, and joy of the child; producing from pleasure and therewith causing delight. The open, honest attitude toward life, springing from desire for power and unity in the soul; attributes to be gained only by the straight look. *Who taught modesty*—the compromise of moderation —to such a child; offspring of the greater mind of man united to a passive, reverential attitude toward it on the part of the conscious mind—*night and sleep?* In waking to the artificial manner of life which a child is expected to adopt, will Innocence dissimulate those joys that must be hidden from the partial mind, or was it perhaps really awake when all this mystery was imposed upon the creations of God? Will Theotormon choose this hypocritical modesty rather than recognize those impulses and desires of human nature which wish fearlessly to declare themselves? If so, then the soul, whose very being is the struggle of impulses to attain to self-knowledge and unity of aim, can be only a *whore* and those pure delights, which had seemed to be an expression which illuminated the nature of the soul, must be only *harlots.* The compulsion to unite all personality under the conscious mind, so that man may in this limited manner attain to unity and wisdom, can be only *a sick man's dream.* The soul in such case is but the *crafty slave,* or instrument, of a unity sought for selfish ends. But this is not true of the soul. *Oothoon is not so.* The soul is spontaneous, virgin, filled with imaginations congenial to its own nature; therefore pure; *fixing its eyes*—seeking to gain perception—wherever they are drawn by the experience of beauty, whether this *appear in the morning or in the evening*— the dawn of an experience still to be comprehended or retrospect over one whose meaning has been discerned.

But there is only one moment in which the soul can act purely and creatively. That is the moment of Desire. Full and free and spontaneous impulse toward production is alone that holy will from which a higher birth may proceed. The creative power checked from expression natural to it will turn to abnormal—*enormous*— *pleasures.* Or there will be generation—only images unfit for exposure to the light. Is it not such repression of which religion is guilty and has not abnormality been the result?

There have been some strange interpretations of this passage on the part of even sensitive readers of Blake's poetry. They must be explained, I think, by two facts. One that the prophecy has not been apprehended in the integrity of its form and meaning— as when the poet's attack upon formal religion and all manner of rationalizing is understood and noted while, at the same time, a defence of free love, in the sexual sense, is inferred. Blake never is guilty of such confusion of issues as that. The other fact is, failure to note the exactness with which Blake selects and uses words. As when *enormous* is read as synonymous with *supreme*, instead of being given its etymological meaning of *contrary to the norm*—a sense in which Blake uses the word in other of his prophecies.

It is, indeed, a pertinent question why in this poem Blake's imagery approached the sensual so much more nearly than in any other; but to particularize his thought in order to make it a plea for free love, is both to forget that Blake in his art never left the impersonal plane of spiritual energy and to fail to grasp this poem as an organic structure. Its author is not putting before us a drama of the life of the soul and preaching a specific social doctrine, both at the same time. There is nothing in any of Blake's writings to justify such a supposition.

In the invective against *Jealousy* and in the acclamation of love as the only motive power strong enough to free the soul, one must realize a man fighting for his life. It has been said that Blake did not know the passions of ordinary men. If that be true it is because he knew intenser passions. He fought—not to possess himself of something of value, whether honours, wealth or love—but to preserve that bright and flaming genius which was the heart and the core of his personality, his "deep eternal self"; and the foes in the moral world within, or the social world without, which threatened this essential thing were as actual and as gigantic to him as any opponent in physical warfare is to the ordinary man. Through the jealousy which lies at the heart of every self-exalting institution, every closed system, that beauty of the world present to a soul left free to assume its burden as the inner life prompts, fades away and the gentle soul becomes *darkened*, an *outcast* from the universal order; a *shadow* dissociated from reality; fearful of losing its identity. Jealousy indeed *preaches* Love, but *can that be love which* holds the soul in thraldom, spinning about it a web that is the product of past ages and that prevents individual expression and growth *till the eyes sicken* at the spectacle of the whole order that exists; its origins in perverted instinct; its development along lines of anti-human tendency; its fruit—the contemporaneous state of the world? This paraphrase is a free one but leans for support upon Blake's well-known philosophy and upon other passages in which the thought that underlies this verse is more clearly developed.

The antithesis of this mode of procedure which jealousy dictates, is perfect and entire freedom for the mind to find beauty and truth where these exist for the soul. *Dear delight* will prove purity. The state will be one of generous love; love that goes out to all that is akin to itself. It is only to such liberality of spirit that the lineaments of the human in external nature appear and the universe becomes animate and spiritual. To *the miser* the sun will never *walk in glorious raiment* before his inner vision or *the cloud drop its* fructifying *moisture* upon the inert part of his nature. His *eye cannot behold the beam* which passes out of the essence of any object and falling upon *the eye of pity* causes it to *expand* — an actual physical occurrence. Never can the miser will to understand the hard labour of *the ox in the plough*. No power of imagination exists, where the mind is bent upon selfish gains, to identify oneself with another being. But the *mild beam of pity*—exacting of another nothing to be added to its own account—*blots out* traits of things that to the narrow mind seem dark and evil. This broad sympathy, this love free from dictation, fearlessly meets the elemental things: The *wintry blast* is *a covering for the wings of the sea fowl*, not a force of merely devastating aim. *Pestilence, poison from the stagnant fen* is the very *adornment of the wild snake*. Trees and beasts and birds become an unfailing source of joy because their own joy is realized as an eternal element in life. There is in Nature this great affirmation of the value of life—an ever young and fresh response to the creative impulse at the heart of the world. Oothoon invokes this spontaneous spirit of free and natural things:

> Arise, you little glancing wings, and sing your infant joy!
> Arise and drink your bliss, for everything that lives is holy.

When Nature so accepts and affirms life shall the soul turn away in pessimistic doubt? It can do no other unless understanding come to the mind.

But Theotormon *sits upon the margined ocean* — the infinite bounded—*conversing with shadows dire* and *the Daughters of Albion hear Oothoon's woes and echo back her sighs.*

Like *Tiriel* and like *Thel*, the poem closes on a note of despair. What is so impervious as rationalistic conviction?

This is the end of this publication.

Any remaining blank pages are for our book binding requirements and are blank on purpose.

To search thousands of interesting publications like this one, please remember to visit our website at:

http://www.kessinger.net